W9-AYF-586

RALLY CARS

by Jeffrey Zuehlke

Lerner Publications Company • Minneapolis

For Graham—quick on all surfaces

Cover Photo: Finnish driver Mikko Hirvonen kicks up dirt around a turn during the 2006 Rally Australia.

Copyright © 2009 by Lerner Publishing Group, Inc.

All rights reserved. International copyright secured. No part of this book may be reproduced, stored in a retrieval system, or transmitted in any form or by any means—electronic, mechanical, photocopying, recording, or otherwise—without the prior written permission of Lerner Publishing Group, Inc., except for the inclusion of brief quotations in an acknowledged review.

Lerner Publications Company
A division of Lerner Publishing Group, Inc.
241 First Avenue North
Minneapolis, MN 55401 U.S.A.

Website address: www.lernerbooks.com

Library of Congress Cataloging-in-Publication Data

Zuehlke, Jeffrey, 1968-
    Rally cars / by Jeffrey Zuehlke.
        p.   cm. — (Motor mania)
    Includes bibliographical references and index.
    ISBN 978–0–8225–9428–4 (lib. bdg. : alk. paper)
    1. Rally cars—Juvenile literature. 2. Automobile
rallys—Juvenile literature. I. Title.
TL236.4.Z84 2009
796.7'3—dc22   2008025571

Manufactured in the United States of America
1 2 3 4 5 6 – DP – 14 13 12 11 10 09

Norwegian driver Petter Solberg powers his Subaru Impreza WRC rally car through a water splash during the 2008 FIA Rally Mexico. Water, sand, dirt, rocks, and high cliffs are all part of the danger and excitement of rally racing.

What Is a Rally?

Rallying is a unique motor sport. Its rules are very different from those in most kinds of racing. World Rally Championship events take place over several days. During that time, the cars may travel hundreds of miles on public roads.

Stages

Each rally is divided into stages. There are three main types.

1. **Special stages** are the parts of the rally where the cars are let loose on closed-off public roads. Each team drives through the stage as fast as possible. The special stages make up the heart of the rally.

2. **Super special stages**, or spectator stages, are held in specially prepared locations, such as sports stadiums *(left)* or on blocked-off city streets. The rally organizers create special tracks. Fans in the seats or on sidewalks get a close-up view of the action.

3. **Transit stages** are the routes that connect the special stages. The cars travel on normal public roads with local traffic. The teams must obey all traffic laws and speed limits. Otherwise, they receive a penalty (usually a loss of time). A team can't win a rally on a transit stage. But a mistake or a rules violation can lose one.

Stages and Timing

Most forms of racing involve many cars competing side by side. Rallies are time trials. The cars take off one at a time, a few minutes apart *(right)*. Each car is timed for the special stages and super special stages. The car that completes the stage the fastest is the stage winner. Every stage time is added to the total for the rally. The driver with the fastest overall time is the winner.

Driver and Codriver

Rally cars seat two people—the driver and codriver *(left)*. The codriver's job is to prepare pace notes for the rally. The pace notes work as a kind of instruction book for how to run the race. As the car screams through the stages at top speed, the codriver calls out the pace notes—for example, "Sharp right turn 50 meters [164 feet]," "Loose gravel patch 100 meters [328 feet]," "Hairpin turn ahead." The codriver is always thinking a few steps ahead. This allows the driver to focus on the moment.

Chapter One

RALLY CAR HISTORY

The first cars appeared in the late 1800s. Inventors in Europe and the United States built their own versions of four-wheeled, self-powered vehicles.

By the late-1890s, a few dozen companies were building cars for sale to the public. They looked for ways to get the public's attention. The most popular way was to have the cars compete in races. Racing was also a way for automakers to test their cars under harsh conditions. There is an old saying, "Racing improves the breed." Competition pushes automakers to try to keep up with their rivals. It forces them to try new ideas and technology. The result is a better "breed" of car.

The very first cars, such as this French-built Panhard-Levassor, were slow, wobbly, and unreliable. But that would soon change.

The Beginning

The sport that came to be known as rallying started in Europe in the late 1800s. The earliest events were called trials. They tested a car's ability to handle difficult conditions. They were also a test of a driver's skill on tricky roads.

One of the first trials was the Automobile Run through South Tyrol, Italy. Held over three days in August 1898, it ran through part of the Alps, a mountain range in central Europe. Three cars competed in the race, which covered 289 miles (465 kilometers) of winding mountain roads.

The competing cars were very basic. The most powerful one had an engine that produced 7 horsepower. (Horsepower, or hp, is a unit used to

As cars became faster and sturdier, they were able to cover longer distances. The picture above shows a 1,000-mile (1,609 km) race held in Great Britain in 1900.

BREAKNECK SPEED?

Dr. Edward Suchanek rode along on the Automobile Run through South Tyrol in 1898. His description of the experience shows how much automobile performance has improved over the last century: "After having covered the first hairpin bends at a comparatively moderate pace, this was soon increased to tremendous racing speed on the straight downhill road. . . . The speed of this wild chase must have been at least 40 kilometers [25 miles] per hour."

measure an engine's power.) A modern-day lawn mower engine produces about the same amount. Obviously, the cars weren't fast. They struggled just to chug up the steep mountain roads. But the race wasn't about speed. It was a test to see if the cars could handle such a tough trip.

Along the way, the automakers learned some important lessons. For example, two of the cars had used leather belts to deliver the engine's power to the wheels. (The belts worked much like the chain on a bicycle.) But the belts broke several times during the event. In response, the automaker began using sturdier chain belts on its cars.

Trials and Rallies

In the following years, many more events took place across Europe. Some were called trials. In 1911 the small country of Monte Carlo held its first event. The event was called the Monte Carlo Rally.

Meanwhile, automobile technology was improving. As the cars became more reliable, the events became longer and tougher. For example, the 1912 Alpine Trial (later renamed the Alpine Rally) covered 1,468 miles (2,363 km). Yet many of the cars were tough enough to finish.

To make things more challenging, organizers created new rules. For example, each car had to reach certain spots on the route within a certain amount of time. If a car arrived too late, the driver lost a few points from his score sheet. At the same time, arriving too soon also earned a penalty. So the key to winning was to reach the end with a "clean sheet."

Rallying—and all other kinds of racing—came to a halt during World War I (1914–1918). More events took place in the 1920s and 1930s. Several rallies became yearly events. They included the Monte Carlo Rally, the Royal Automobile Club (RAC) Rally Great Britain, and the Alpine Rally.

The Monte Carlo Rally

The Monte Carlo Rally is the world's most famous rally. The Monte Carlo Rally was first run in 1911 and was the first event to be called a rally.

The event is held every January and has some unique challenges for drivers. Most of the route runs through the mountains of southern France. (The event begins and ends in Monte Carlo. But most of the route runs through southern France.) Its narrow, winding asphalt roads are tricky to drive. And the high mountain air often produces snow. So the rally teams don't know what to expect from stage to stage.

The Monte Carlo Rally also starts in a unique fashion—the short opening stage takes place at night. Equipped with powerful headlights, the cars speed through the French forests.

Drivers line up their cars at the start of the 1912 Monte Carlo Rally.

The 1950s:
A Changing Sport

The sport began to change following World War II (1939–1945). By this time, the FIA was overseeing most forms of European auto racing. The organization set down the same rules for all rallies.

Rally cars of the 1950s were not much different from ordinary road cars. The best ones were usually sports cars, such as the Porsche 356 and the Mercedes-Benz 300SL. Many of these cars were lightweight and fast. They used a front-engine, rear-wheel-drive layout. (The engine was mounted toward the front of the car and powered the rear wheels.)

As the sport grew in popularity, several countries began holding their own rallies. The Acropolis Rally ran through the rocky terrain of Greece. The 1000 Lakes Rally wound through the forests of Finland. Both were summer events. On the other hand, the Rally to the Midnight Sun took place on the ice and snow of Sweden.

Meanwhile, more automakers were joining the fun. Alfa Romeo (Italy), Porsche (Germany), BMC (Great Britain), Saab (Sweden), and many other companies used rallying to showcase their cars.

Salvador Fabregas speeds his Mercedes-Benz 300SL during a nighttime special stage of the 1956 Monte Carlo Rally.

The 1960s: Factory Teams

The competition was heating up. So automakers formed "works" (factory) departments to oversee their racing efforts. These works teams included some of the world's smartest engineers. They worked day and night to improve their cars' performance.

But the factory teams couldn't just build and race any kind of car. Each model of car had to be homologated (approved) by the FIA. The rules kept the teams from making too many changes to the cars. For example, a Saab V4 rally car had to be very similar to the Saab V4 road car. The FIA let teams change some parts to improve performance. But both road and rally cars had to have the same engine and basic design. The homologation rules helped to balance the competition.

Despite these rules, the cars kept improving. The front-engine, rear-wheel-drive layout had always ruled the rallies. Then, in 1960, a tiny car from Great Britain turned the rallying world upside down. The Mini Cooper S looked boxy and awkward. But it was quick and very nimble.

The key to the Mini's success was its front-engine, front-wheel-drive layout. Front-wheel-drive gives a car better control than rear-wheel-drive. (It's easier to control something when you pull it rather than push it.) The Mini's engine was mounted over the

This Saab V4 rally car looks nearly identical to the road version. Part of the appeal of rallying is that fans get to watch race cars that look much like the cars they own themselves.

front wheels. All that weight on the front wheels gave the car great traction. The Mini didn't have a high top speed. But it could scoot through turns much faster than heavier cars. The Mini's great handling helped it win the Monte Carlo Rally three times in the 1960s.

Meanwhile, a handful of rally drivers were earning success and fame. Fans followed the events to see how their favorite drivers were doing. In the 1960s, drivers such as Rauno Aaltonen, Timo Mäkinen, Paddy Hopkirk, and Pat Moss became racing celebrities.

The 1970s: Rallying Goes Worldwide

By the 1970s, rallying had grown beyond Europe. The grueling East African Safari Classic ran through Kenya, Uganda, and other East African countries. The Morocco Rally swept through the deserts of North Africa. The United States, Canada, and New Zealand also held rallies during the decade.

At the same time, Japanese automakers joined the action. Toyota, Mitsubishi, and Datsun (the company that later became Nissan) sent cars to compete.

Rallying had truly become a worldwide sport. So in 1973, the FIA created the World Rally Championship for Manufacturers. Automakers battled it out for the title of world champion. (The FIA would create a championship for drivers six years later.)

As the sport grew, the factory teams kept trying new ideas. They put bigger engines in the cars. They toughened up the cars' chassis and suspension systems. (The chassis is the basic frame

The Mini Cooper defied convention as it raced to the top of the rally car standings in the 1960s.

of the car. The suspension is the set of parts that connect the wheels to the chassis.) These changes allowed drivers to push the cars harder and faster.

Yet rally machines of the early 1970s were still just modified road cars. That is, until Italian automaker Lancia tried something different. In 1974 Lancia introduced the Stratos. This amazing machine was the first car built especially for rallying. The Stratos looked nothing like other rally cars. It was very short and low to the ground. The car's low, wedge-shaped front end made it very aerodynamic. This means it cut through the air very easily.

Inside, the Stratos's machinery was even more amazing. It had a mid-engine, rear-wheel-drive layout. The Stratos's 240 hp engine was mounted

The Stratos

The Lancia Stratos (right) is probably the most popular rally car of all time. It was the star of the show at every rally. In 1974 journalist Peter Newton described the Stratos at the RAC Rally Great Britain:

"A deep musical throb grows among the trees, then with a bark of triumph, the Stratos leaps out of the gloom into the sunlight . . . the red and white [rocket] hurls itself at the straining watchers on the corner. The sheer speed of its arrival takes everyone by surprise."

behind the driver and codriver. This put most of the car's weight on the rear wheels, giving it fantastic traction.

Lancia's "supercar" competed in its first world championship rally in 1974. It won easily. Many more wins would follow over the next several years. The Stratos carried Lancia to three straight championships beginning in 1974.

The Stratos took rallying to a whole new level. Fans flocked to see this amazing car in action. It was beautiful, fast, and exciting to watch. And its Ferrari engine made a mighty roar.

Homologation Rules

The FIA's homologation rules weren't just designed to level the playing field. They are also supposed to keep the cost of racing from getting out of control. For example, if a large automaker wants to spend huge amounts of money on its racing program, smaller companies may struggle to keep up. And if racing becomes too expensive, then automakers won't want to participate.

Production numbers are a key to the homologation rules. In order to race a car in FIA events, automakers must build a certain number of cars exactly like it for sale. For example, in 1969 Ford homologated its Escort Mk I for rallying. In order to race, Ford had to show that it was going to build 1,000 copies of the ordinary road version of the Escort. (The numbers have changed many times over the years.) The rules made sure that the cars didn't stray too far from production models. Few companies could afford to build so many cars just for racing (although Lancia would later do just that with the Stratos).

In the 1980s, the FIA dropped the required number to just 20 cars for the Group B class. This allowed the automakers to really experiment with their rally cars. The result was the most exciting— and dangerous—years of WRC history.

1980s: The Group B Cars

The Stratos was in a league of its own. Lancia had gone all out to build it. No other automaker was willing to spend so much money on its rallying program. But in the 1980s, the FIA changed the rules to allow teams to try new ideas.

For the first time, the FIA allowed four-wheel-drive cars. The extra traction of four-wheel-drive was perfect for rallying. Audi of Germany was one of the first companies to race a four-wheel-drive car. Walter Röhrl drove his turbocharged Audi Quattro to the title in 1982. The Quattro blew away the competition and changed rallying forever.

The following year, the FIA made more rule changes. It created a special class of cars called Group B. Teams could do just about anything they wanted with their Group B cars. This included using turbocharged engines. (A turbocharger is a device that uses a car's exhaust gases to create extra power.) Some teams also copied the Stratos's mid-engine, rear-wheel-drive layout.

During the next few years, automakers produced faster and more powerful cars. The Peugeot 205 Turbo, Lancia Delta S4, and Renault 5 Turbo were all turbocharged, mid-engine monsters. The Peugeot's engine produced a whopping 500 hp! These supercars were fast and agile. They were a thrill to watch, and they drew huge crowds at every rally.

In fact, the cars were too fast. Drivers struggled to handle them. Meanwhile, the crowds of spectators were growing out of control. Rally organizers couldn't keep people off

The rear-engine Peugeot 205 Turbo was a powerful Group B car that roared to the top of the pack in the 1980s.

One of the exciting parts of watching rallying is getting close to the action. But sometimes people get too close—a danger to both the spectator and the driver.

the roads. This frightening mix of too much speed and too many people was a recipe for disaster.

At the 1986 Portugal Rally, the crowds got out of control. Three people were killed after being struck by a rally car. Another tragedy followed a few months later. At the Corsica Rally, popular Finnish driver Henri Toivonen lost control of his Lancia Delta.

His car slid off a cliff and burst into flames. Toivonen was killed, along with his codriver, Sergio Cresto.

The FIA acted swiftly. It banned Group B just hours after Toivonen's crash. Mid-engine supercars were outlawed. The most exciting period in World Rally Championship history had come to a sad end.

The 1990s:
Group A and WRC Cars

Many fans were unhappy to lose the Group B cars. Rally car racing continued, although its popularity dipped. In the 1990s, the top WRC class was Group A. These turbocharged, four-wheel-drive cars were less powerful than the Group B supercars. They were safer to drive but not as thrilling to watch.

Meanwhile, Japanese cars began to move to the forefront of the sport. European automakers had ruled the rallies since the beginning. Japanese cars had won many events, but no Japanese company had won a championship. That changed in 1993 when Finnish driver Juha Kankkunen drove his Toyota Celica Turbo to the title. Toyota's title began a string of titles for Japanese companies. Over the next seven seasons, the manufacturers' championship changed hands between Toyota, Subaru, and Mitsubishi.

Ladies and Gentlemen

Women have been competing in rallies since the beginning. Records show that a Miss Helene Morariu-Andriewitsch competed in the Alpine Trials of 1912 and 1913. Soon after, the Alpine Trial created a special award just for women drivers.

Beginning in the 1950s, a handful of women made their mark on the sport. The most famous among them was British driver Pat Moss. The sister of racing superstar Stirling Moss, Pat made her own name driving for the British Motor Corporation (BMC). She and codriver Ann Wisdom won several major rallies in the 1960s. The pair helped pave the way for other women drivers in the sport.

The most successful female rally driver of all time is Michelle Mouton *(below right)*. The fiery Frenchwoman is the only woman to win a WRC event. In fact, she and female codriver Fabrizia Pons *(below left)* won four rallies driving for Audi in the 1980s. In 1982 Mouton nearly won the WRC title. She fell short when her car went off the road in foggy conditions at the second-to-last rally of the season.

Finnish driver Tommi Mäkinen drives his Mitsubishi during the Tour of Corsica rally in 2000.

European drivers kept a stranglehold on the drivers' championship, however. Kankkunen won two of his four titles in the 1990s. In 1995 Colin McCrae became the first British driver to win a WRC title. Tommi Mäkinen of Finland won the next four titles. In fact, no non-European has ever won a WRC title.

Flying Finns

When it comes to producing great rally drivers, Finland truly stands out. The first great Finnish rally drivers were Rauno Aaltonen and Timo Mäkinen *(below)*. Nicknamed the Flying Finns, they were two of the top drivers of the 1960s and 1970s. Many other Finns have followed in their footsteps. They include world champions Juha Kankkunen, Tommi Mäkinen, Hannu Mikkola, Ari Vatanen, and Marcus Grönholm. In fact, from 1979 to 2007, Finnish drivers won 13 out of 29 WRC titles. By comparison, French drivers have the second-most titles, with just five.

The WRC-Car Era and Beyond

In 1998 the FIA replaced Group A with a new class of car—World Rally Car. The new cars are fast, safe, and exciting. From the outside, they look like normal road cars. But inside, they are completely rebuilt for rallying. They are fitted with the latest technology, including 300-hp engines and strong roll cages that protect the drivers during crashes. They also moved the gear shifter onto a wheel-mounted paddle, allowing the drivers to keep their hands on the wheel while shifting.

In 2000 French automaker Peugeot finally ended Japan's run of manufacturers' titles. The company's top driver, Marcus Grönholm, joined the list of legendary Finnish world champions.

Peugeot and Subaru ruled the early 2000s. In 2004 another French company joined the fight. The Citroën Xsara WRC would prove to be one of the all-time great rally cars. In the hands of Sébastien Loeb, it would be almost unbeatable. Beginning in 2004, Loeb and codriver Daniel Elena stormed to four straight WRC titles. Along the way, Loeb shattered nearly every WRC record, including all-time wins, most wins in a row, and most rally wins in a season.

The humble Frenchman's speed and flawless style make him exciting to watch. Loeb's success has drawn even more fans to this very special and thrilling sport.

Sébastien Loeb and codriver Daniel Elena compete in a WRC Rally in Mexico in 2008. *Inset:* Sébastien Loeb poses during the Jordan Rally in 2008.

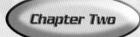

Chapter Two

RALLY CAR CULTURE

The World Rally Championship is truly a worldwide sport. WRC rallies have been held on every continent except Antarctica. New Zealand, Japan, Argentina, and Mexico are just a few of the countries that have hosted WRC events. Fans around the globe love to watch the action, both in person and on TV or the Internet.

Yet the heart of the sport remains in Europe. More than half of each year's rallies take place there. All the factory teams are based in Europe. Even the Japanese companies base their rally programs in Europe to stay on top of this fast-moving sport.

The Season

Rally team members joke that the season never ends. This is not far from

Mikko Hirvonen powers his Ford Focus WRC through the mud on his way to winning the 2007 Rally Great Britain.

the truth. The season begins in Monte Carlo in January. It ends with the RAC Rally Great Britain in late November or early December. Over a full season, the teams compete in 16 countries.

Each event has its own special challenges. But rallies can be roughly divided into three different types. The types are based on the rally route's surface. Asphalt rallies, such as the Monte Carlo Rally, run mostly on paved roads. Gravel or dirt rallies, such as Rally Mexico, take place on rocky, unpaved roads. Snow events, such as Rally Sweden, run over snow- and ice-covered trails. (Many rallies have a mix of two or more types of surfaces.)

Asphalt rallies usually run on narrow, winding roads. The paved routes tend to be easier on cars than gravel roads. But drivers need to go flat out (as fast as possible) on every stage. They must control their cars with pinpoint accuracy. A small mistake can

The Dakar Rally

The world's most famous rally is not a WRC event. In fact, it's not really even a rally. The Dakar Rally is actually an off-road endurance event. It is one of the toughest tests of human and machine ever created.

First run in 1978, the early events were called the Paris-Dakar Rally. They ran from Paris, France, to Dakar, Senegal, on the west coast of Africa. In recent years, the starting point was changed to Lisbon, Portugal. The race's brutal route ran through the blazing heat and sand of the Sahara. The cars, trucks, and motorcycles covered thousands of miles over several days. Yet hundreds of people—both professional and amateur—enter the race every year.

In 2008 the rally was canceled after terrorists threatened to attack the racers. The event organizers decided to move the rally to the desert regions of Chile and Argentina for 2009. But the name of this famous race remains the same.

cost the team valuable seconds. A big mistake can send the car off the road and into a tree—or off a cliff.

Gravel events make up most of the WRC schedule. Rocky, dusty roads are brutal on cars. Tire punctures are common. And if a car hits a stray rock in the road, the damage can knock the car out of the rally. A driver's feel for the road is key to success on gravel. The driver must slide the car through turns, judging how well the tires are gripping the road. If the car hits the turn too fast, it may spin or flip. If the driver is too cautious and slow, the car will lag behind the competition.

Snow events are the toughest of them all. Blasting over narrow, snowy roads at 100 miles (161 km) per hour takes a lot of skill and courage! Freezing temperatures add to the difficulty. Again, the driver's feel for the surface is key. The driver must be able to judge how fast the car can go without losing control. Snow rallies are also tough on cars. The routes are usually lined with tall snowbanks. The white snowdrifts may look soft. But they feel like brick walls when cars smash into them.

Andreas Mikkelsen of Norway sees his race come to a painful end when he flips his Ford Focus during the 2007 FIA Wales Rally Great Britain.

Rallies

Most rallies take place from Friday through Sunday. (Monte Carlo begins on a Thursday night.) But the work begins days in advance. The teams arrive the weekend before the event. They set up shop in the service area. This is a large area such as a stadium, arena, or parking lot.

The service area is like a large campground. The teams eat and sleep in motor homes parked nearby. The service area has everything the teams need to work on the cars. Fans can visit the park to watch the mechanics in action.

The driving begins on Tuesday or Wednesday. Teams get two days to do reconnaissance, or recce, when they study the course in detail. The driver follows the course while the codriver writes pace notes. The codriver makes notes on road conditions, length and sharpness of turns, and any special

Citroën team mechanics work on Sébastien Loeb's C4 at a service area during the 2008 Monte Carlo Rally. Fans watch the progress from a gallery (right).

hazards. Getting the pace notes right is crucial for success during the rally. If the codriver gives the wrong instructions, the car could end up off the road.

The rally itself begins on Friday morning. The event often kicks off with a super special stage. These short, spectator stages draw big crowds. They are a way for the drivers and the crowd to get warmed up for the event.

The real racing takes place during the special stages. Some special stages are short sprints of just a few miles. Others last for a few dozen miles. The drivers go flat out in a race against the clock. Crowds line the stages to see the cars fly down the road. Fans can get within a few feet of the cars.

If a car crashes or breaks down on a special stage, the driver and codriver are on their own. They must repair the damage, limp the car home, or drop out of the rally. The crews carry a few tools and spare parts for simple repairs.

Driver Jan Kopecky reviews the pace notes before the Wales Rally Great Britain in 2006.

Small service areas are set up along the route. Special rules apply to working in these areas. The teams are given a set amount of time (often 45 minutes) to fix and adjust the cars. Only a handful of mechanics are allowed to work on the cars. If the car needs a lot of repairs, the driver and codriver pitch in. The teams can carry only certain replacement parts, so major rebuilds are out of the question.

The FIA keeps track of each special stage time. The stage winner is the team that finishes the stage the fastest. After each stage, the FIA adds the numbers to see who is leading the

DID YOU KNOW?

Drivers and teams earn points based on their results in each rally. At the end of the season, the driver and the team with the most points wins the title. Here's how the points are awarded.

Winner: 10 points

2nd place: 8 points

3rd place: 6 points

4th place: 5 points

5th place: 4 points

6th place: 3 points

7th place: 2 points

8th place: 1 point

overall rally. If a team breaks a rule—such as staying in the service area after their time has run out—the FIA may hand out a time penalty. The penalty will add a few seconds or minutes to the team's overall time.

The event concludes on Sunday afternoon or evening. The final stage is often another super special. This is an extra treat for the fans—a chance for the drivers to show off their skills in front of roaring crowds.

Rally Cars

World Rally Cars are state-of-the-art racing machines. Every part of the car

Fan Participation

Fans don't just watch rallies. Sometimes they participate! If a car flips over or lands in a ditch, spectators will come to the rescue. They help the team flip the car over or push it out of a ditch *(below)*. If a driver gets lost or loses track of the route, the fans are usually happy to give directions. Fan participation isn't always a good thing, though. People sometimes try to slow down or knock out cars by throwing rocks or ice on the route. Such behavior is unsportsmanlike and dangerous.

is made to deliver maximum performance under brutal conditions.

To build a car for WRC racing, the teams begin with a normal factory car. They strip every part from the body shell and strengthen the shell with extra welding. The teams also cut holes in the hood. These openings allow the engine to suck up plenty of air. The holes also allow heat to escape, keeping the engine cool.

The teams totally remake the inside of the car. They remove the seats, carpet, interior panels, and accessories. Then they install seats made of strong carbon fiber. The seats are molded to fit the driver and codriver perfectly. They work as a protective shell in case of crashes.

The roll cage is another safety feature. These are structures made of steel tubes. They protect the driver and codriver from being crushed in an accident.

Under the hood, World Rally Cars feature turbocharged, four-cylinder

Tires: Getting a Grip

WRC teams use tires that are made just for rallying. Tires can play a big part in winning—and losing—these races. Tire makers—such as Pirelli, BFGoodrich, and Michelin—often produce several different kinds of tires for each event. The teams must choose the tires that will work the best in the current conditions. For example, softer tires stick to the ground better than harder tires. They give the car better traction and control. But harder tires last longer.

Tire companies make special tires (*right*) for snow rallies. The tires are just a few inches wide. Snow tires have hard metal studs for extra grip.

engines. For safety reasons, FIA rules limit engine power to about 300 hp. Rally cars can reach top speeds of about 150 miles (241 km) per hour.

DRIVING SIDEWAYS

Some people say rally car drivers are the most skilled racers in the world. Roger Clark, a British rally legend of the 1970s, describes sliding his car down the road at high speed: "I don't care how far sideways I am. As long as I'm not actually looking out of the back window, I should be able to get [the car] back in line."

But top speed isn't the key to rally success. Going around so many turns and bends, the cars rarely have a chance to get going very fast. Quick acceleration, or picking up speed, is the important thing. The car needs to be able to come out of a turn and get going quickly. A World Rally Car can go from 0 to 60 miles (96 km) per hour in about three seconds.

Drivers

WRC drivers are some of the best—if not *the* best—drivers in the world. So what does it take to be a WRC driver? Experience helps. Many WRC drivers began racing go-karts or other vehicles long before they earned their drivers' licenses. They spend years honing their skills to a world-class level. But not everyone has been at it since childhood. For example, four-time world champion Sébastien Loeb ran his first rally at the age of 21.

To handle long, punishing rallies, drivers must be physically fit. WRC drivers train year-round. Training programs include riding bicycles, long-distance running, and swimming.

All professional rally drivers work hard. But talent and instincts are what separate the good from the great. Drivers need quick hands and feet to work the car's pedals and steering wheel. Having a feel for the car is also important. A driver will use his eyes, ears—and even his rear end—to feel how the car is performing. The best drivers just have a knack for knowing how hard they can push their car without crashing.

A driver must also be cool under pressure. Every driver makes mistakes. The key to success is to minimize the damage. Clipping a tree or wall at top speed can be a shocking experience. But the best drivers can shrug off their mistakes and keep going. They're tough, just like the racing machines they drive. Their skill is what keeps the fans coming back for more.

Rallying in the United States

Rallying has been a popular sport in the United States since the 1970s. The Sports Car Club of America (SCCA) organized the first major U.S. rallies. Growing interest in the sport led the FIA to organize WRC events in the United States in 1973 and 1974. Not long after, the SCCA organized the PRO Rally national championship.

During the late 1970s, the PRO Rally title belonged to one man—John Buffum. The greatest U.S. rally driver of all time, Buffum has won 117 national rallies and seven PRO Rally championships. In the 1980s, he became the first—and only—American to win a European championship event. On top of his amazing driving skill, Buffum also has a photographic memory. He can remember every detail of every stage route. This ability has been a big part of his success.

The WRC returned to the United States in the mid-1980s, running events from 1986 through 1988. In the 1990s, several Japanese companies supported rallying in the United States. Subaru, Mitsubishi, and Hyundai all used the sport to show off their cars.

Professional rallying continues to grow in the United States in the 2000s. The country is home to two national championship series, Rally America and the U.S Rally Championship. Founded in 2002, Rally America organizes about nine national events per season. The popular series features U.S. rallying's biggest stars, including Ken Block and 2006 and 2007 champion Travis Pastrana. Beginning in 2006, the series organized a rally as part of the X Games, a popular ESPN event. With its thrills and danger, rallying fits in perfectly with the X Games other extreme sports.

Travis Pastrana races to a dramatic win at the 2006 X Games.

The World Rally Championship

The World Rally Championship travels thousands of miles every year, to every corner of the globe. The events change from year to year. This world map shows the schedule from recent seasons. Each inset map* shows the three legs of each course for the 2008 season. The first leg is shown with a dashed black line, the second leg with a green line, and the third leg with a red line.

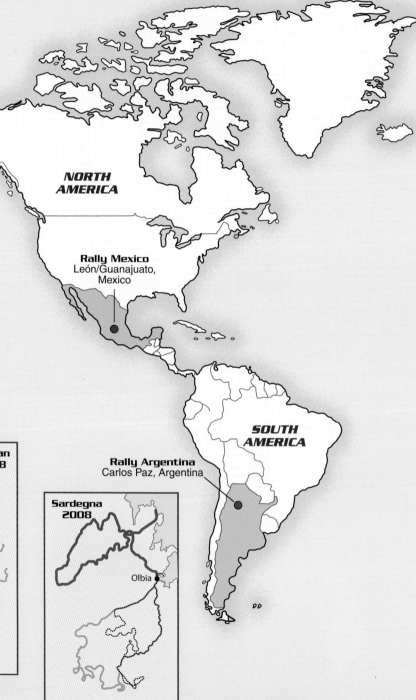

NORTH AMERICA

Rally Mexico
León/Guanajuato, Mexico

SOUTH AMERICA

Rally Argentina
Carlos Paz, Argentina

Tallard

Rosans

Monte Carlo 2008

Monte Carlo

Sweden 2008

Karlstad

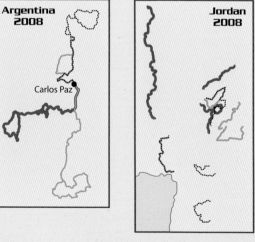

León

Guanajuato

Mexico 2008

Argentina 2008

Carlos Paz

Jordan 2008

Sardegna 2008

Olbia

*The inset maps are not drawn to scale.

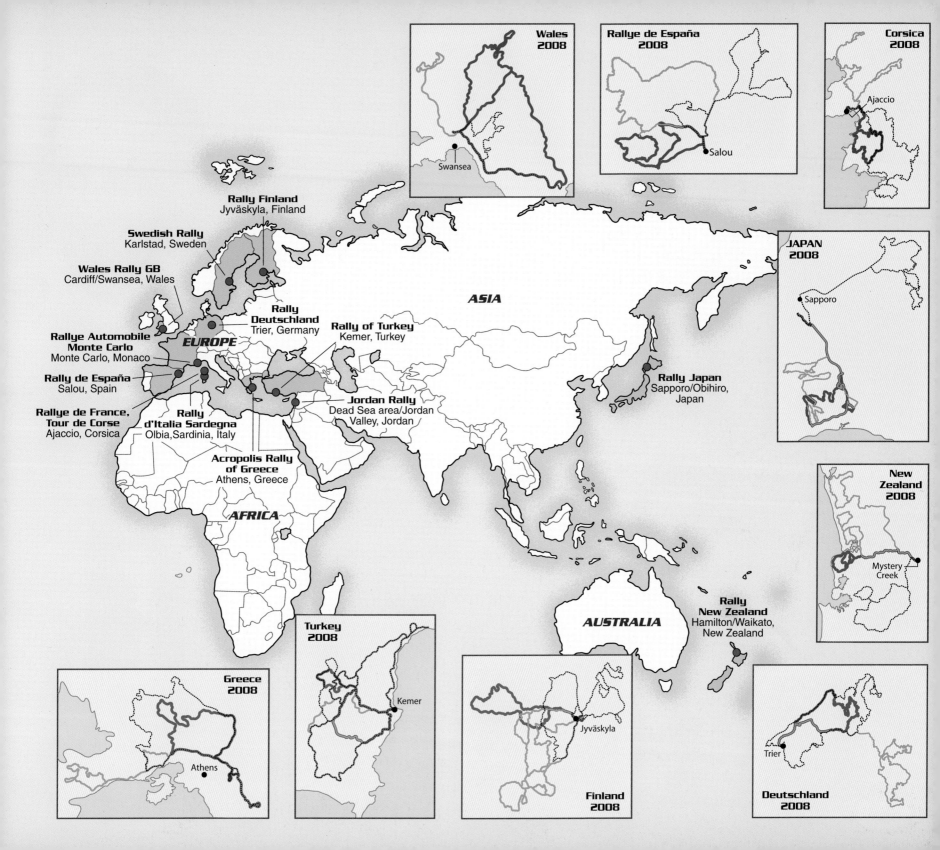

Wales 2008
Swansea

Rallye de España 2008
Salou

Corsica 2008
Ajaccio

JAPAN 2008
Sapporo

New Zealand 2008
Mystery Creek

Rally Finland
Jyväskyla, Finland

Swedish Rally
Karlstad, Sweden

Wales Rally GB
Cardiff/Swansea, Wales

Rally Deutschland
Trier, Germany

Rally of Turkey
Kemer, Turkey

Rallye Automobile Monte Carlo
Monte Carlo, Monaco

Rally de España
Salou, Spain

Jordan Rally
Dead Sea area/Jordan Valley, Jordan

Rallye de France, Tour de Corse
Ajaccio, Corsica

Rally d'Italia Sardegna
Olbia, Sardinia, Italy

Acropolis Rally of Greece
Athens, Greece

Rally Japan
Sapporo/Obihiro, Japan

Rally New Zealand
Hamilton/Waikato, New Zealand

ASIA

EUROPE

AFRICA

AUSTRALIA

Greece 2008
Athens

Turkey 2008
Kemer

Finland 2008
Jyväskyla

Deutschland 2008
Trier

Miki Biasion (born 1958)

Miki Biasion was the first Italian to win a WRC title. He enjoyed his greatest success driving for Lancia in the late 1980s. A smart and skillful driver, Biasion used a steady approach. He drove as fast as he needed to, but he was rarely out of control. The Italian usually brought his car home in one piece, racking up 17 wins and two titles along the way.

Nationality: Italian

Seasons: 1981–1994

WRC wins: 17

Championships: 2 (1988, 1989)

Stig Blomqvist (born 1946)

Blomqvist spent much of his career driving for Saab. But his greatest success came driving the Audi Quattro Group B cars. In 1984 he crushed the competition, winning five races and the title. He scored his final win in 1984. Yet his love for rallying kept him going. He continued to race in the WRC on a part-time basis until 2006.

Nationality: Swedish

Seasons: 1969–2006

WRC wins: 11

Championships: 1 (1984)

Miki Biasion,
Lancia Delta HF Turbo, 1987

Stig Blomqvist, Audi Quattro Turbo, 1984

Marcus Grönholm (born 1968)

Tall, lanky Grönholm was the only man who could keep up with Sébastien Loeb in the mid-2000s. Before that, Marcus Grönholm was the man to beat, winning two titles with Peugeot in 2000 and 2002. He and codriver Timo Rautiainen dominated their home rally. The pair won Rally Finland a record seven times. Grönholm retired after the 2007 season.

Nationality: Finnish
Seasons: 1989–2007
WRC wins: 30
Championships: 2 (2000, 2002)

Juha Kankkunen (born 1959)

Kankkunen was the first driver to win four WRC titles. He grew up on a farm near Jyväskylä and was driving cars and tractors by the age of seven. He scored his first win driving a Toyota Celica in 1985. From there he would change teams several times, winning titles for Peugeot, Lancia, and Toyota.

Nationality: Finnish
Seasons: 1979–2002
WRC wins: 23
Championships: 4 (1986, 1987, 1991, 1993)

Marcus Grönholm, Ford Focus WRC, 2007

Juha Kankkunen,
Toyota Celica Turbo,
1993

Sébastien Loeb (born 1974)

Is Sébastien Loeb the greatest rally driver of all time? Many people think so. The cool, calm Frenchman is already the most successful driver in the sport's history. In 2006 he shattered the record for the most WRC wins. The following year, he won his fourth straight championship, and he shows no signs of slowing down.

Nationality: French

Seasons: 2001–

WRC wins: 36

Championships: 4 (2004–2007)

Tommi Mäkinen (born 1964)

Tommi Mäkinen and his red Mitsubishi Lancer Evo ruled the WRC in the late 1990s. The key to his success was his skill on all surfaces. He was as good on the asphalt of Monte Carlo (four wins) as he was on the ice of Sweden (three wins). Like so many other Finnish drivers, he got his start driving tractors on the family farm.

Nationality: Finnish

Seasons: 1990–2003

WRC wins: 24

Championships: 4 (1996–1999)

Sébastien Loeb,
Citroën C4, 2008

Tommi Mäkinen,
Mitsubishi Lancer Evolution,
1997

Colin McCrae (1968–2007)

Fans loved Colin McCrae because he never gave up. His many accidents earned him the nickname Colin McCrash. But he usually found a way to drag his car home—even if he did lose some pieces along the way. He spent the best years of his career driving for Subaru, winning the title in 1995. His death in a helicopter crash in 2007 was a huge blow to the rallying world.

Nationality: British

Seasons: 1989–2006

WRC wins: 25

Championships: 1 (1995)

Walter Röhrl (born 1947)

Called a genius on wheels, German driver Walter Röhrl has won both rallies and sports car races. He drove for many teams during his career. He won his first WRC title driving for Fiat in 1980. Two years later, he won again, driving for German automaker Opel. He went on to win several races for Lancia and Audi before retiring in 1987. He still competes in sports car races, driving for Porsche.

Nationality: German

Seasons: 1979–1987

WRC wins: 14

Championships: 2 (1980, 1982)

Colin McCrae, Subaru Impreza, 1998

Walter Röhrl, Audi Quattro Turbo, 1984

Carlos Sainz (born 1962)

The two-time world champion was nicknamed El Matador by his Spanish fans. As tough and brave as a bullfighter, Carlos Sainz was also a bit unlucky. Mechanical failures robbed him of titles in 1991 and 1998. Both came in the last race of the season. The most painful loss was in 1998, when his car broke down 500 yards (457 m) from the finish. Yet Sainz's 26 wins was the WRC record until Loeb broke it in 2006.

Nationality: Spanish
Seasons: 1987–2005
WRC wins: 26
Championships: 2 (1990, 1992)

Petter Solberg (born 1974)

The cheerful Norwegian is one of the WRC's biggest stars. Petter Solberg grew up in a racing family and helped repair cars as a kid. He got his chance in the WRC after winning the Norwegian national championship in 1998. He soon showed he was a world-class driver. He joined Subaru in 2000 and won the title three years later. His brother Henning is also a popular WRC driver.

Nationality: Norwegian
Seasons: 1999–
WRC wins: 13
Championships: 1 (2003)

Carlos Sainz,
Citroën Xsara WRC, 2004

Petter Solberg, Subaru Impreza WRC, 2005

Ari Vatanen (born 1952)

The charming and handsome Finn was one of rallying's biggest stars in the 1970s and 1980s. Fans loved his all-out driving style. He tended to crash a bit too often, but that just made him more exciting to watch. A major accident in 1985 almost cost him his career—and his life. But he returned the next season to win the Monte Carlo Rally. Since retiring from driving, he has enjoyed a career in politics.

Nationality: Finnish
Seasons: 1974–1998, 2003
WRC wins: 10
Championships: 1 (1981)

Björn Waldegård (born 1943)

Björn Waldegård was one of the greatest rally drivers of the 1970s. The son of a Swedish farmer, he began competing in national rallies in the early 1960s. In 1975 Lancia offered him the chance to drive its Stratos supercar. He responded with a win his first time out. Many more wins would follow in a variety of car models. In 1979 he won the first WRC driver's championship.

Nationality: Swedish
Seasons: 1969–1991
WRC wins: 16
Championships: 1 (1979)

Ari Vatanen, Peugeot 205
Turbo, 1985

Björn Waldegård, Ford Escort, 1977

Glossary

chassis: the main frame of a car. The engine, suspension, and bodywork are all connected to the chassis.

codriver: a person who sits next to the driver and helps the driver by reading off notes about the rally route

pace notes: notes about the rally route that have been prepared by the codriver before the rally

recce: sessions that take place before the rally during which the driver and codriver are allowed to explore the course and draw up notes about the rally route

roll cage: a set of strong bars that surrounds a car and protects the driver during a crash

service area: a large area where rally teams set up and repair their cars before and during the rally

service areas: areas along a rally route where a small number of team members are allowed to repair the cars during the rally

special stages: sections of the rally on closed-off public roads through which the driver and codriver try to pass as fast as possible

super special stages: stages of a rally that are usually held in stadiums or city streets where fans can see all the action

suspension: the set of parts that connect the wheels to the car's chassis

transit stages: sections of a rally where the teams drive along with normal traffic and must follow all local traffic laws

Selected Bibliography

Arnold, Ronnie. *American Rally Action 2*. Flower Mound, TX: SPEED-PICS Publishing, 2007.

Gardiner, Tony. *RAC Rally Action!* Dorchester, UK: Veloce Publishing, 2005.

Hope-Front, Henry, and John Davenport. *The Complete Book of the World Rally Championship*. Saint Paul: Motorbooks International, 2004.

Pfundner, Martin. *Alpine Trails & Rallies*. Dorchester, UK: Veloce Publishing, Ltd., 2005.

Robson, Graham. *Austin-Healey 100-6 & 300*. Dorchester, UK: Veloce Publishing, 2007.

———. *Ford Escort Mk. I*. Dorchester, UK: Veloce Publishing, 2006.

———. *Lancia Stratos*. Dorchester, UK: Veloce Publishing, 2006.

———. *Subaru Impreza*. Dorchester, UK: Veloce Publishing, 2006.

Williams, David, ed. *Rallycourse 2002–2003*. Richmond, UK: Hazelton Publishing, 2002.

Further Reading

Doeden, Matt. *Sports Car Racing*. Minneapolis: Lerner Publications Company, 2009.

Raby, Philip. *Racing Cars*. Minneapolis: Lerner Publications Company, 1999.

Savage, Jeff. *Travis Pastrana*. Minneapolis: Lerner Publications Company, 2006.

Websites

Rally America
http://www.rally-america.com/index.php
The official website of Rally America features rally reports, information on rallying, and profiles of the best drivers.

Sébastien Loeb Official Website
http://www.sebastienloeb.com
Visit the website of the WRC's all-time winningest driver.

WRC.com
http://www.wrc.com/index.jsp
The official World Rally Championship website features schedules, news, video clips, and more.

Index

About the Author

Jeffrey Zuehlke has written more than two dozen books for children, on subjects ranging from muscle cars to Poland to Henry Ford to Joseph Stalin. He lives in Saint Paul, Minnesota.

About the Consultant

Jan Lahtonen is a safety engineer and auto mechanic. He has raced sports cars and worked as a performance driving instructor. He has followed car racing for more than 40 years.

Photo Acknowledgments

The images in this book are used with the permission of: © Luis Acosta/AFP/Getty Images, pp. 4–5, 21, 39 (top); © Louisa Gouliamaki/AFP/Getty Images, p. 6; © McKlein Photography, p. 7 (top); © McKlein/LAT Photographic, pp. 7 (bottom), 21 (inset), 22 (background), 26, 38 (top), 42 (top); © National Motor Museum/Topham-HIP/The Image Works, p. 8; © Edgar Scamell/Hulton Archive/Getty Images, pp. 8 (background), 9; © Branger/Roger Viollet/Getty Images, p. 11; © LAT Photographic, pp. 12, 13, 14, 15, 17, 18, 34 (both), 35 (both), 37 (bottom), 41 (bottom), 44 (both), 45 (both); © Mike Powell/Allsport/Getty Images, p. 19; © Olivier Laban-Mattei/AFP/Getty Images, p. 20 (top); © Evening Standard/Hulton Archive/Getty Images, p. 20 (bottom); © Adrian Dennis/AFP/Getty Images, p. 23; © Damien Meyer/AFP/Getty Images, p. 24; © Bryn Lennon/Getty Images, p. 25; © Drew Gibson/LAT Photographic, p. 27; © Robert Cianflone/Getty Images, p. 28; © Grazia Neri/Allsport/Getty Images, p. 29; © Ben Liebenberg/WireImage/Getty Images, p. 31; © Laura Westlund/Independent Picture Service, pp. 32–33; © Reporter Images/Getty Images, pp. 36 (top), 43 (both); © Howard Boylan/Allsport/Getty Images, p. 36 (bottom); © Bertil Ericson/AFP/Getty Images, p. 37 (top); © Allsport/Getty Images, p. 38 (bottom); © Hardwick/LAT Photographic, p. 39 (bottom); © Jeff Bloxham/LAT Photographic, p. 40 (top); © Gabriel Duval/AFP/Getty Images, p. 40 (bottom); © Phil Walter/Getty Images, p. 41 (top); © Clive Mason/Getty Images, p. 42 (bottom).

Front Cover: © Tony Ashby/AFP/Getty Images.

Source Notes

10 Martin Pfundner, *Alpine Trails and Rallies: 1910–1973* (Dorchester, England: Veloce Publishing Limited, 1973), 7.

15 Graham Robson, *Lancia Stratos* (Dorchester, England: Veloce Publishing, Ltd., 2006), 60.